greeting card magic
with RUBBER STAMPS

MaryJo McGraw

NORTH LIGHT BOOKS
CINCINNATI, OHIO
www.nlbooks.com

about the author

MaryJo McGraw is a nationally known rubberstamp artist whose work has been featured in leading rubberstamp-enthusiast publications. She has taught rubberstamp classes for over 11 years at stamp stores around the country and has conducted demonstrations and classes at all the major national retail stamp shows.

MaryJo has been a sample artist for many of the largest stamp manufacturers in the country and has sold her original artwork to several art-stamp companies. She currently works for JudiKins in Gardena, California.

Greeting Card Magic With Rubber Stamps. © 2000 by MaryJo McGraw. Manufactured in China. All rights reserved. No part of this book may be reproduced in any form or by any electronic or mechanical means including information storage and retrieval systems without permission in writing from the publisher, except by a reviewer, who may quote brief passages in a review. Published by North Light Books, an imprint of F&W Publications, Inc., 1507 Dana Avenue, Cincinnati, Ohio 45207. (800) 289-0963. First edition.

Other fine North Light Books are available from your local bookstore, art supply store or direct from the publisher.

04 03 02 01 00   5 4 3 2 1

Library of Congress Cataloging-in-Publication Data
McGraw, MaryJo
  Greeting card magic with rubber stamps / by MaryJo McGraw.
    p. cm.
  Includes index.
  ISBN 0-89134-979-0 (pbk. : alk.)
  1. Greeting cards. 2. Rubber stamp printing. I. Title.
TT872.M34 2000
745.594'1—dc21   00-020010

Editors: Jane Friedman and Nicole R. Klungle
Designer: Stephanie Strang
Production coordinator: Emily Gross
Production artist: Donna Cozatchy
Photographer: Christine Polomsky

METRIC CONVERSION CHART		
To Convert	**To**	**Multiply By**
Inches	Centimeters	2.54
Centimeters	Inches	0.4

acknowledgments

THANK YOU

to all the friends, stamp store owners and stamp company owners

who are so generous with their time, talent, ideas and products

throughout the year. I would especially like to thank the students

I meet traveling around the country each year. Your thoughts,

questions and creativity keep stamping interesting for me.

....

I'd also like to thank my brothers,

Art, Tim, Matt and Mark Uvaas,

for helping me with all the little day-to-day

stuff that comes up. It makes my life a little

easier knowing I can count on you guys.

Thanks.

table *of* contents

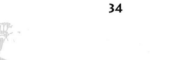

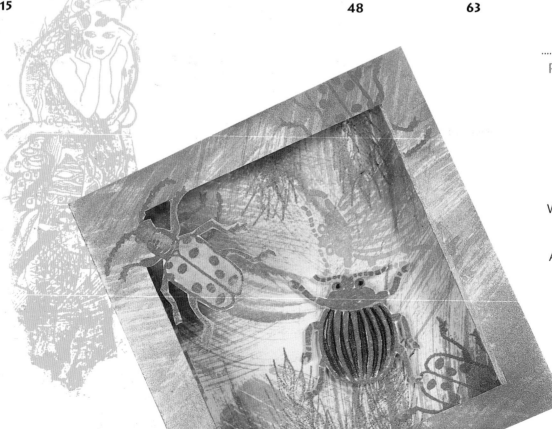

8

9

Creative Rubberstamping Techniques looked at some interesting techniques with many staple items that stampers use today. Those ideas were meant as an introduction to using mixed media on greeting cards. I hope in this book to dive a bit deeper into that same pool of creativity.

introduction

Many of the ideas in this book can be taken even further than the greeting card. Again I will use some items that are familiar: paper, metallic pens and embossing powders. The unusual—acetate, glazing glue, shrink plastic, laminating sheets and templates—will become familiar quickly. These items are all easy to use and create fabulous effects on cards. Be adventurous! Use these techniques on other surfaces too. Limiting yourself to using only paper for your creations will obstruct your creativity. Expand beyond the greeting card onto other surfaces, such as cardboard frames, wooden boxes and even your windows and walls.

Above all else, PLAY! *All of these techniques are simple and easily mastered with a bit of practice. Get out all your craft and stamping stuff and* ENJOY!

Tools and Materials

Rubber stamps
There are generally three parts to a rubber stamp: the mount, the cushion and the die. Quality mounts are made from hardwood. The cushion is made of foam from ⅛" to ¼" thick. The die, the most important part of the stamp because it transfers the design, should be closely trimmed.

Paper
Most of the projects in this book require high-grade papers and cardstock. Don't skimp on the paper—it will show. One of the papers you need to find is a translucent vellum. Be sure you can see through it, as there are many types of vellum that are opaque.

Inks
There are three basic ink types: dye, pigment and solvent. Dye-based pads are the type you see lying around the house or office. Dye-based ink is water-soluble. Pigment inks are now widely available through stamp and gift stores and are a good choice when using uncoated papers. They are also used for embossing and for archival applications, such as scrapbooking. Solvent-based inks are used mainly for stamping on unusual surfaces like wood, plastic and ceramic. I use them for a nice, crisp, black outline that won't smear like dye inks do.

Dye re-inkers
Dye re-inkers are the small bottles of ink you normally use to refill your dye-based ink pads. In this book they will be used to color Diamond Glaze: By adding a few drops of re-inker to Diamond Glaze, you can make a paint that dries transparent. Be careful when using inks straight from the bottle; they are very concentrated and will easily stain clothing. Be sure to use the smallest amount possible; you can always add more.

Embossing powders
Embossing powders are required for many of the cards in this book. To use embossing powder, stamp an image with pigment or embossing ink. Sprinkle the powder over the wet ink and shake off the excess. Use a heat gun to melt the powder and create a raised design. Be sure to have a variety of colors; embossing looks great in almost any color. Embossing powder comes in solid-color and multicolor forms.

Double-sided tapes
Double-sided tapes come in a variety of forms. The double-sided tapes used in this book include mosaic tape, a paper-lined tape that is thin, embossable, heat resistant and good for layering. Cellophane double-sided tape is also great for layering, especially with transparent papers. Double-sided foam tape is perfect when you need to add height to a layered piece.

Accessories
Accessories such as threads, beads, paper cord, tassels and gift tags can be found at most stamp stores. I also find these items in specialty stores for beads and needlecrafts. Office supply stores are great for unusual items too.

Acetate
The acetate used in this book can be found in stamp stores. You want to be sure to get embossable acetate (also known as "window plastic") in case you want to heat the piece. The same is true of the heavy cold laminate used here; it should be embossable. The thicker the laminate is, the better for the projects in this book because of the beating the pieces will take.

Beads
The glass beads I use in the projects in this book are tiny and have no holes. They also have a metallic finish.

Bone folder

The bone folder is a great tool for scoring paper and smoothing down creases. Bookbinders use it for turning corners and scoring. Some are made from bone, while others are made from resin or wood. They come in several lengths and are very helpful in several crafts.

Brayers

Brayers come in so many varieties it is hard to choose which to buy. For my money, the best all-around brayer is a detachable 4" soft rubber brayer. It will handle most jobs and it is easier to clean. You will also find sponge, acrylic, hard rubber and wood brayers. Each yields a different result.

Craft knives

A craft knife is an invaluable tool when creating greeting cards or other stamp projects. The blade should be pointed and very sharp. Change your blades often to ensure clean cuts.

Heat gun

Look for a heat gun that is specially made for stamping: They are usually geared at a safe temperature for paper projects. Keep your heat gun away from your cutting mat, as it can distort the surface. (It's hard to cut on a warped mat.)

Pastels and water-soluble crayons

Pastels and water-soluble crayons are available in stamp and art supply stores. I prefer crayons that are soy based because they have a creamy texture and are loaded with pigment.

Powdered pigments

Powdered pigments are raw pigments used for a variety of purposes, including making your own paints. You can also use these pigments as a surface coating on paper or collage projects. Powdered pigments do need what is known as a "binder" to keep them adhered to your project. In this book we will be using Diamond Glaze as a binder. Other options include white glue, paint mediums, gum arabic or spray fixative. Mixing any of these with the powdered pigments will create a colored medium you can apply to surfaces as you wish.

Shrink plastic

Several projects in this book call for shrink plastic, so I want to give you some tips for using it. Most shrink plastics shrink by 40 to 50 percent. You can shrink the plastic using a heat gun on a heat-safe surface (not your cutting mat), but be aware that the heat will not be even over the piece and consequently the plastic may become distorted.

You can also shrink the plastic in your oven. To ensure distortion-free results, place the plastic in a hot spot. It is easy to test your oven for hot and cold spots. Create several 1-inch squares of shrink plastic. Place these squares on a parchment-covered cookie sheet, spreading the pieces evenly on the sheet. Be sure to put a piece in each corner. Place the cookie sheet in a hot oven, and watch through the oven door to see which pieces begin to shrink first. This will tell you where your oven hot spots are. That is where to place the pieces you are shrinking.

Tassels and cords

Tassels make a great addition to a beautiful card. The ones used in this book are available at most stamp stores. Paper cord is also available. As you will see in this book, paper cord is an extremely versatile decorative item. Both tassels and cords are usually sold in assortments of colors.

Templates

Plastic and brass templates are a great investment. They last forever, are inexpensive, and there are many types available. Look for envelope, box and card templates at stamp stores.

CHAPTER

1

(STAMPS CLOCKWISE FROM LEFT) Rubber Moon, Stampers Anonymous, JudiKins.

pockets and mini envelopes

$\mathcal{E}$veryone loves a little surprise. The cards in this chapter feature built-in pockets and

envelopes for mysterious correspondence. The basics are simple folds and the use of

envelope templates, which are perfect for those tiny messages. These are great cards for

extravagant embellishments: silk, velvet, gold or specialty threads and small charms or

tags. You might also enclose a pair of earrings or a gift certificate in the envelope.

Basic Envelopes With Templates

What you'll need:

- vellum
- envelope template (see page 14)
- bone folder
- white glue
- envelope glue (see recipe on page 14)

For this envelope I have used a type of vellum that is tinted but transparent. There are many colors available. Some even have embedded glitter or confetti. You should be able to find this at your local stamp, craft or paper store.

Materials, clockwise from upper left: stamped and unstamped papers and vellum, gift tags, envelope templates, bone folder, craft knife, cutting mat.

1 *Trace the envelope template.* Begin by tracing the template lightly onto the vellum with a pencil.

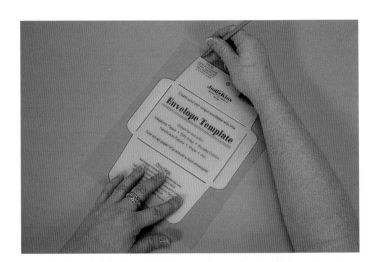

2 *Score the vellum.* Using a bone folder or a stylus, score the vellum using the slots in the template.

3 *Cut out the envelope.* Cut out the envelope along the pencil lines. Remove any pencil marks with a soft eraser.

4 *Fold the envelope.* Fold along the score marks and burnish the creases with the side of the bone folder.

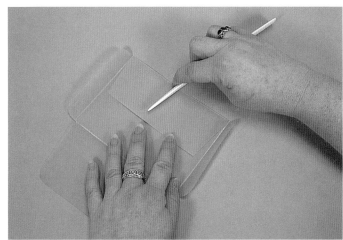

5 *Glue the seams.* Using a paintbrush and a small amount of clear-drying glue, cover the lower half of the envelope seams. Fold and seal the seams. Do not use this glue for the envelope flap.

T I P

☆ Recycle old magazines, calendar pages and gift wrap into new envelopes. For a more personal envelope, copy your family photos on a color copier!

6 *Apply envelope glue.* Using the recipe on this page, make a batch of "lickable" envelope glue. Apply the glue to the top flap of the envelope.

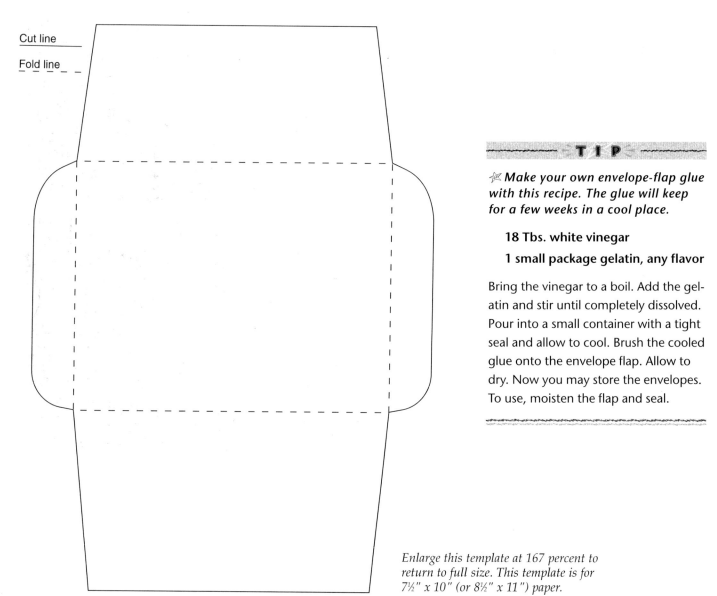

Cut line _____

Fold line _ _ _

Enlarge this template at 167 percent to return to full size. This template is for 7½" x 10" (or 8½" x 11") paper.

Mini Message Card

What you'll need:

- small round stamp from JudiKins
- rectangular stamp from Stampers Anonymous
- word stamp from Zettiology
- brown paper—text weight
- tall notecard
- round gift tag
- white glue
- mini square envelope template
- pencil
- bone folder
- scissors
- metallic embossing powder
- heat gun
- gold thread
- double-sided tape
- metallic pigment ink
- black and green dye inks

1 *Make a mini envelope.* Stamp plain brown light-weight paper with black dye ink. Trace the mini square envelope template following the basic envelope instructions on pages 12–14. Score and cut out the envelope. Set it aside.

2 *Make a liner.* To make a liner for the envelope, use a pencil to trace the square interior through the template slots. Continue tracing around the top flap. Cut along the pencil lines.

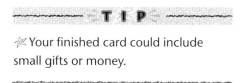

TIP

⭐ Your finished card could include small gifts or money.

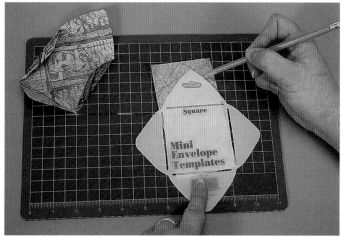

3 *Attach the liner.* Trim ¼″ off the liner on all sides and glue the liner to the inside of the envelope. Glue the seams of the envelope and set it aside.

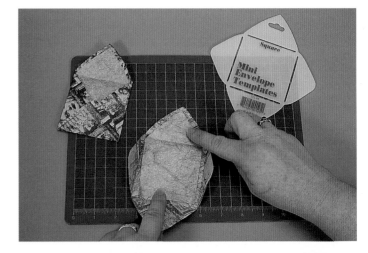

4 *Dye the tag.* Color the tag with dye ink. Wipe off any excess ink on the metal rim of the tag. Allow to dry.

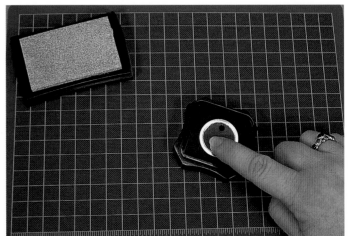

5 *Stamp the tag.* Stamp a design on the tag with pigment ink. Again wipe away any excess on the rim with a paper towel.

TIP

✐ Many types and sizes of tags are available at your local office supply store.

6 *Add embossing powder.* Sprinkle embossing powder over the wet pigment ink and shake off the excess.

7 *Emboss the tag.* Use a heat gun to heat the embossing powder until it melts.

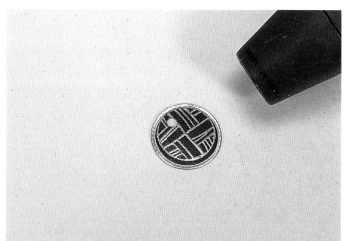

8 *Make the mini card and finish the mini envelope.* Using the template, trace just the inside square and cut it out. Trim this piece as necessary to fit inside the envelope perfectly. Write or stamp your message on the card and slip it in the envelope. Wrap gold thread around the envelope several times and tie on the tag. Trim away excess thread with scissors.

- - - - - **T I P** - - - - -

✂ Raffia, yarn and narrow ribbons also work well for trims on greeting cards. Be sure to keep the size of the trim in proportion to the card.

9 *Attach the envelope to the card.* If you wish, stamp the tall notecard along the edge with a coordinating design. Apply the piece to the front of the card with any double-sided tape.

The finished card and enclosure.

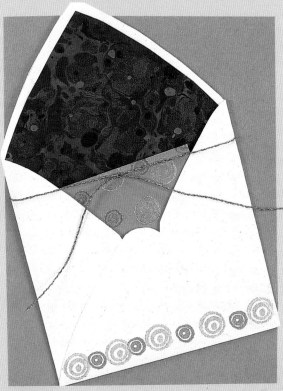

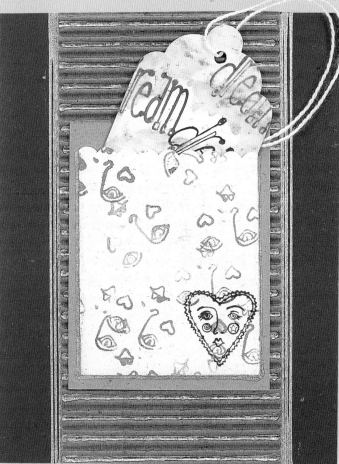

CHAPTER 2

Queen of Last Minute

diorama cards

Rubber stampers have been making diorama cards for many years. They are wonderful cards to receive and unique enough to treasure as a keepsake of holidays, birthdays and vacations. Although the card looks complicated, the use of a template makes the whole process fast and easy.

Doggy Diorama

What you'll need:

- dog stamps by Rubber Zone
- butterfly stamps by Claudia Rose
- 11" x 17" cardstock in your choice of color
- diorama template
- watercolor crayons or pens
- black dye ink
- bone folder
- double-sided masking tape
- craft knife

Create a theme by selecting stamps of similar styles or subjects. Here I have chosen a set of active dogs. Landscape and collage stamps work well for dioramas.

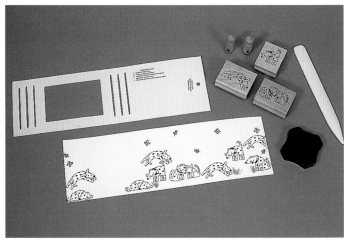

Materials, clockwise from upper left: diorama template, stamps, bone folder, ink pad, cardstock (already cut and stamped).

1 *Cut cardstock, stamp image and score.* Cut a piece of cardstock-weight paper to the size of the template. Stamp the characters in black dye ink. After the ink has dried, lay the template back over the paper and use a bone folder to score through the slots.

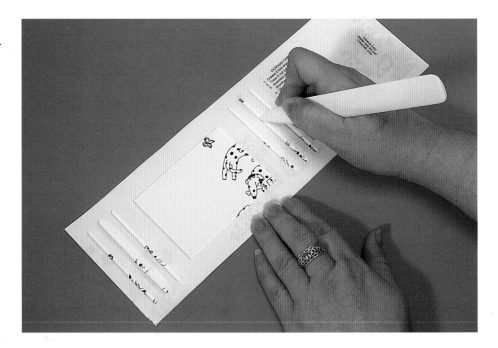

T I P

✄ If you have a hard time holding the template and paper together, use removable tape to secure the two pieces, score them, then remove the tape.

---

2 *Mark the window area.* With a pencil, mark out the window area of the template.

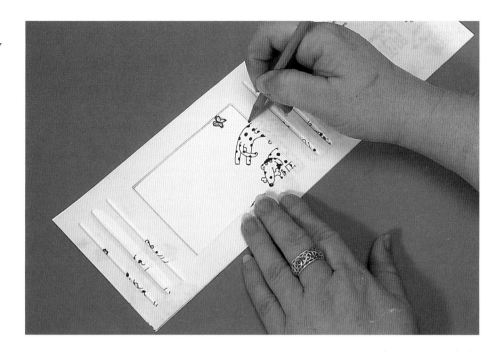

3 *Add extra elements.* Now that you know where the window will be, you can add extra elements jutting out of the window. I have placed the stamp to make it look as if the dog is jumping halfway out of the window.

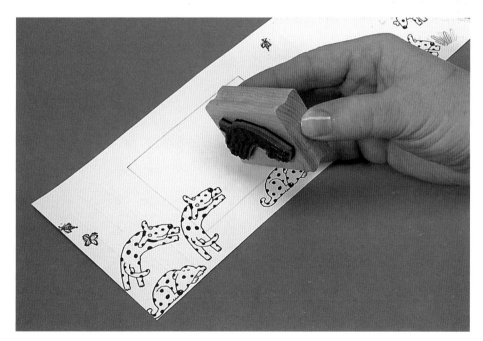

4 *Cut out the window.* Now cut out the window section with a craft knife, being careful to cut around the designs stamped inside the window.

5 *Fold.* Fold the score marks accordion style. Crease each fold with the bone folder. Do not overwork the creases by folding back and forth. The card will stand better with crisp creases.

The folds should look like this from above.

6 *Color the design.* Lay the entire card out flat again and add color to your design with colored pencil, markers, crayons or water-colors.

7 *Finish the card.* Apply double-sided tape to the side seam. Fold the entire card flat to seal it. Trim any uneven edges with a sharp knife—slowly. Change your knife blade before making your final trims.

The finished card.

To add dimension to your diorama, use double-sided foam tape to adhere cutouts to the back of the diorama behind the window.

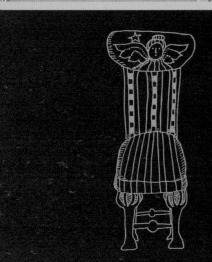

longe inquisitionis l
lectendi cupido incessi
dico uoluminum num·
pos mentis, domestice·
lici superiorum stilo
stantiori facundia·
hinc ... enel qu
... ce rem
... cuius ce

CHAPTER

3

(STAMPS CLOCKWISE FROM LEFT) Rubber Moon, Acey Duecy, Stamp Camp.

cutting corners

$\mathscr{U}$se your tools! That ruler you have can create interesting designs out of paper you have

stamped! These cards can be quick to make, too, because you can cut enough pieces

for several cards in no time. You'll also have plenty of leftovers for emergencies.

Simple Cut-Up

What you'll need:

- rectangular stamp by JudiKins
- cardstock
- pigment ink
- embossing powder
- heat gun
- craft knife
- double-sided tape
- tassel

Though this is an easy technique, most folks who receive this card will be very impressed with your cutting skills.

1 *Stamp your image.* Begin by stamping an image in pigment ink on cardstock.

2 *Emboss the image.* Sprinkle embossing powder over the still-wet ink and shake off the excess. Use a heat gun to melt the embossing powder.

3 *Cut in half.* To start making a pattern, use a sharp craft knife to cut the image in half lengthwise.

4 *Cut in quarters.* Cut those pieces in half again.

5 *Seal the embossing.* Reheat the edges of each piece to reseal the embossing. This will keep the embossing from flaking off along the edges.

6 *Build your card.* Affix double-sided masking tape to the back of each stamped piece. Then layer the pieces onto contrasting cardstock leaving ¼" between the pieces.

7 *Finish and embellish the card.* Finish the greeting by adhering the cardstock to a dark-colored notecard and tying on a matching tassel.

TIP

✯ To create a more intricate pattern, cut the pieces into smaller sections and use several colors of paper or embossing powders.

Tumbling Triangles

What you'll need:

- small stamps by Paula Best
- cardstock
- paper in several colors/patterns
- dye ink
- double-sided masking tape
- 8½" x 11" Cosmic vellum
- hole punch
- tassel

This card is fun, quick and easy to create. Cube stamps work well in this project, since their designs fit well into a square.

1 *Cut squares.* Begin with three different colors of paper. Cut at least three 1½" squares out of each color. Here I have used cinnamon, forest and white.

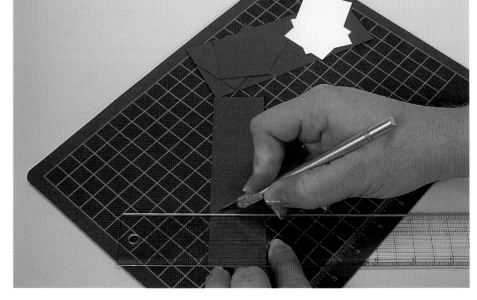

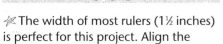

TIP

✎ The width of most rulers (1½ inches) is perfect for this project. Align the edge of your ruler with one edge of the paper, and then slice it on the other side. Repeat for the top and bottom.

2 *Stamp the papers.* Use one color of ink to impress all the squares with different stamp patterns. Allow the ink to dry.

3 *Cut triangles.* Cut the squares diagonally to make triangles.

4 *Stick triangles to card.* Apply small pieces of double-sided masking tape to the backs of the triangles. Position the triangles, alternating the colors, on a tall card.

5 *Make the overlay.* For this card I made a vellum overlay. It goes over the card and tucks under the triangles. Fold a piece of 8½" x 11" Cosmic vellum in half lengthwise and trim to fit the tall card. Unfold the vellum and lay your ruler along the fold so the ruler is on the right of the fold. Cut away the vellum to the right of the ruler, leaving about 1½". Fold the vellum overlay onto the card.

6 *Attach the tassel.* You can attach the overlay with a tassel by punching two holes on the crease of the card and the overlay.

The finished card. If you are making a card for a wedding, try this card using shades of white and cream.

Here are a few examples of alternating different colors of paper. When using this technique, be sure to choose a color of embossing powder that is compatible with both papers. Don't choose a color that is too light.

For these two cards, the stamped and embossed images were stacked, then cut. If you stack the images before cutting them, you'll end up with images that match perfectly across the cut.

CORPUS

CHAPTER 4

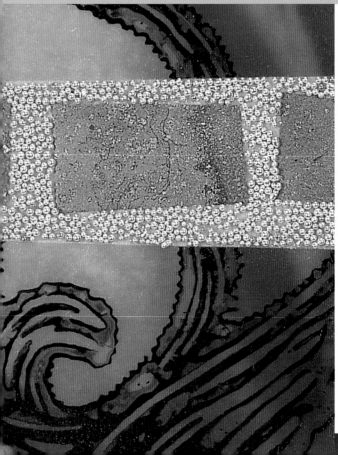

(STAMPS CLOCKWISE FROM LEFT) Stampers Anonymous, American Art Stamp, A Stamp in the Ha

exquisite paper mosaic

This is by far the most rewarding concept I have ever found because literally *everyone* can

do it. Paper mosaic is quick, easy and beautiful. It can look modern, elegant, country or

just pretty. Best of all you can do this project with a variety of paper scraps, including

stamping leftovers or mistakes, magazines, gift wrap and wallpaper—even old photos.

The unfortunate thing is you'll never want to throw any paper away ever again.

Mosaic Technique

What you'll need:

- colorful stamped and unstamped scraps of paper
- double-sided masking tape
- paper cording
- craft knife
- cardstock

All of these cards were made with scraps of paper, double-sided tape and paper cording.

This is hands-down the easiest way to create elegant greeting cards: The lovely patterns you'll create will amaze you. Pull together many types of stamped papers. Include in your selection large stamped backgrounds, metallic or shiny papers, embossed pieces, leftover glazed strips (see chapter five) and anything you were tempted to throw away! Once you have assembled the papers, cut them into strips with your craft knife and ruler. Even strips cut on the diagonal will work. Be sure that all the strips have straight edges on all sides. Sort the strips into color combinations for each mosaic.

1 *Cut mosaic strips.* Use a craft knife to cut strips of colorful, stamped or unstamped paper. Make sure the sides are straight and parallel.

TIP

✍ I like to use at least two patterned or stamped papers for each mosaic—it makes for a much more interesting pattern.

2 *Add strips to tape.* Start with a 4"-long section of double-sided masking tape. Lay the tape sticky side up on your cutting mat. Put one strip of paper at an angle across the center of the tape. Carefully lay another strip next to it, followed by another. Do not trim the strips just yet.

3 *Add cord and perpendicular strips.* Lay a paper cord on either side of the strips and press firmly. Once you have several strips across the center, begin laying strips perpendicular to your original strips.

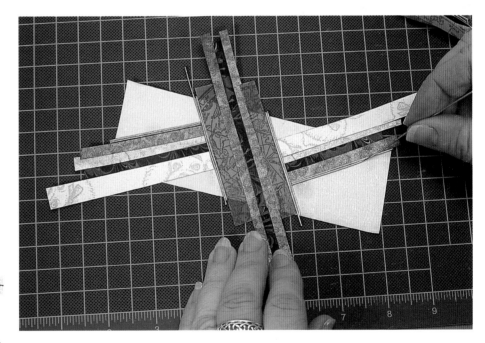

T I P

✐ I prefer to use double-sided masking tape for this project because it is very forgiving. At times, you'll want to move the strips after you've put them on the tape. With this tape, you will be able to do so.

4 *Fill the tape.* Repeat the process until the tape is covered.

5 *Trim the mosaic.* When the tape is covered, turn the piece over with the backing face up. Trim ⅛" off of each side of the tape.

6 *Finish the card.* Peel the liner off the tape and layer it onto cardstock. Trim the cardstock to about ½" around the mosaic. Apply double-sided tape to the back and layer it all onto a tall notecard.

TIP

✐ If you have tape showing between the strips, pour on a contrasting embossing powder to fill the spaces. Shake off the excess and heat. This not only fills in unwanted space, but also gives a tile-like finish. You can also try coating the entire piece with a clear powder like Amazing Glaze.

Deluxe Mosaic

What you'll need:

- a completed mosaic
- craft knife
- double-sided masking tape
- paper cord
- notecard

Now let's create a more intricate piece. By cutting the mosaic into smaller strips, you can create more interesting looks and even patterns.

1 *Make a mosaic.* Begin by completing a mosaic as in the previous project (steps 1 through 5). Before removing the backing of the double-sided tape, cut this piece into four ⅜" strips.

2 *Place strips on tape.* Cut another section of tape long enough to place your newly cut strips on. Remove the liner of each mosaic piece before placing it onto the the sticky side of the second piece of tape.

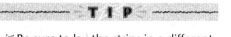

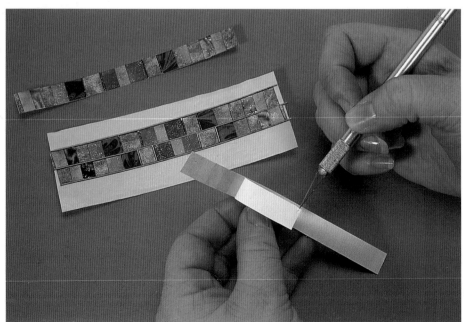

✫ Be sure to lay the strips in a different pattern from which they are originally cut. By turning every other strip you'll achieve a much more eye-catching pattern.

3 *Add cording and finish card.*
Place a paper cord between
each strip. Continue until all four
pieces are in position, and then
trim away the remaining exposed
tape. Peel off the liner and place
directly on a notecard.

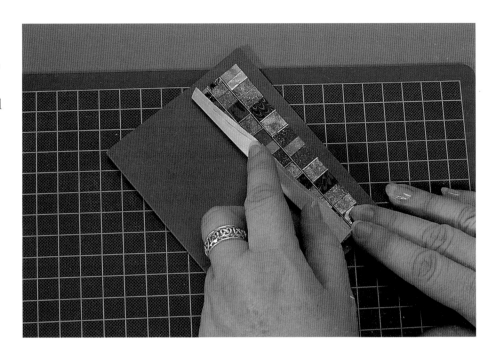

T I P

✻ If you like a glossy finish, spread
Diamond Glaze over the surface of the
mosaic.

The finished card.

Glitzy Mosaic

What you'll need:
- scraps of paper

or
- scraps from the projects in chapter five
- double-sided masking tape
- glass beads
- square notecard

Try the underglazing technique in chapter five and then use the leftover scraps on your latest mosaic. This mosaic uses blue and pink underglazed scraps, but you can use paper scraps with this technique as well.

1 *Arrange mosaic pieces on tape.* Begin with small, square chunks of colored plastic or small leftover paper strips. Here I am using two 4" sections of tape that will create a square-finish mosaic. Place the largest pieces toward the center of the double-sided tape and surround each piece with tiny scraps of strips. Leave ⅛" of exposed tape showing between each piece.

2 *Add glass beads.* In a box lid, lay the tape exposed side up and then pour tiny glass beads over the entire surface. Gently roll the beads over the tape with your fingertips. Lift the tape and tap off any excess beads.

T I P

★ Pour the beads over the surface of the tape instead of turning the tape over and rolling it in the beads. You'll see where the beads should go so you can press them in with your fingers.

3 *Attach mosaic to card.* Remove the liner from the back of the tape and place each piece on the notecard as shown.

T I P

⭐ Make several of these beaded mosaics and put them all together on a piece of matboard. Frame for an interesting piece of abstract art.

The finished card.

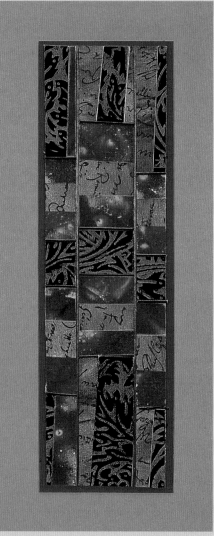

This mosaic was cut in half diagonally, creating two triangles. A spare mosaic strip was used to separate them.

Check out quilting books for some great patterns you can create using this technique.

Tall cards are perfect for mosaic sections, and are very elegant. These cards are perfect for men or women.

As you can see, paper cords add dramatic effect to mosaics. Simply wrapping a cord around a mosaic before layering the mosaic on a card adds lots of texture.

Try small, uniform squares as a central element in a mosaic.

CHAPTER

5

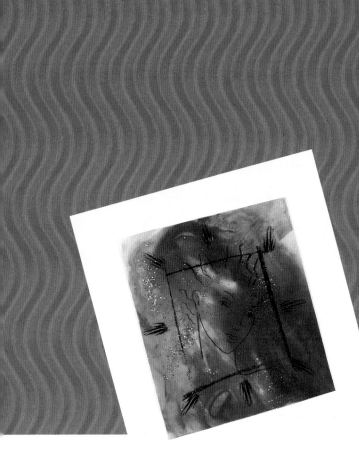

glazing with glue

This is a great idea for those who love a little glitz. Make up several pieces at a time so you'll have extra cards on demand. Underglazing is a technique in which Diamond Glaze and dye re-inkers are used to create a colorful background on the reverse side of transparent acetate. You can also cut these into smaller pieces and add them to your latest mosaic. Overglazing uses a mixture of Diamond Glaze and dye re-inkers to make a transparent, glossy paint.

Pear Card

What you'll need:

- pear stamp from Stampers Anonymous
- word stamp from Zettiology
- clear acetate with tissue liner
- Diamond Glaze
- dye stamp pad re-inkers in several colors
- black permanent (solvent) ink
- craft knife
- ruler (preferably clear)
- double-sided masking tape
- notecard

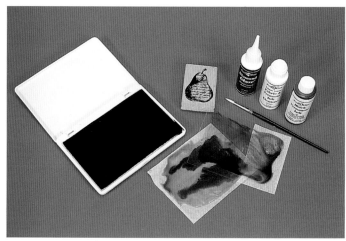

Materials, clockwise from upper left: permanent (solvent) ink pad, stamp, Diamond Glaze, stamp cleaner for permanent ink, permanent ink, a small paintbrush, acetate.

This project uses acetate that is embossable and that usually comes with a tissue liner. Remove the liner and set it aside. In the photo at right the tissue has not been removed so that you can see the plastic.

1 *Add glaze to the acetate.* Squirt on a half-dollar-size amount of Diamond Glaze.

TIP

☆ If you can't find Diamond Glaze, you can substitute the following:

gloss medium

clear-drying glues

Test several colors first—these items may not dry as clear.

Your local stamp or art supply store should carry acetate. You can also find it at:

copy shops

office supply stores

teacher supply stores

2 *Add ink to the glaze.* Open your re-inkers and carefully add a drop or two of ink to the glaze. Let the ink blend into the glaze. Add a couple of drops of another color, allowing the inks to blend. Caution: Adding too much ink can cause the Diamond Glaze to stay soft. A basic mixing ratio is three parts Diamond Glaze to one part ink.

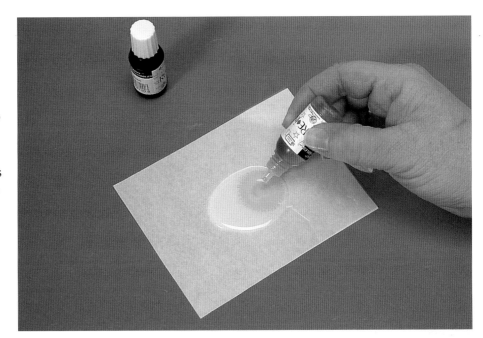

3 *Mix the colors.* If you feel the colors have not meshed well, use a paintbrush to swirl the inks together while the glaze is still very liquid. Do not overmix or the color will become muddy. Spread the mixture over the surface of the plastic.

TIP

✯ Use less ink with deep colors. Barely a drop is plenty.

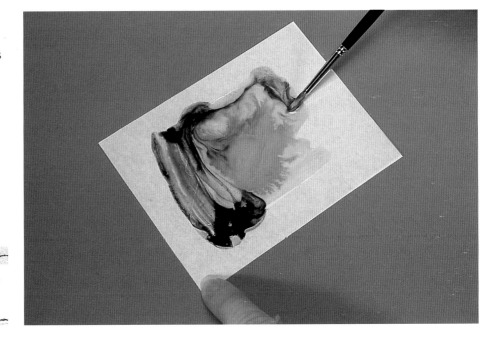

4 *Dry and stamp.* Allow the mixture to dry completely. This should take about 15–20 minutes. (It can take longer in a humid climate.) Once the glue is dry, turn the plastic over and stamp your images with permanent (solvent) ink (dye ink will bead up on the acetate). For this particular technique I like to use dreamy or collage-style images.

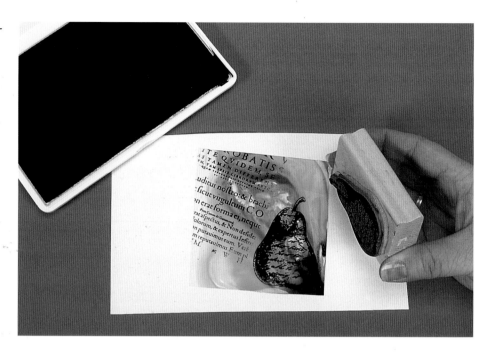

5 *Trim the acetate.* Cut a ½" frame out of a 4" x 4" piece of cardstock using a craft knife and your see-through ruler.

6 *Apply tape.* Center the plastic onto the back of the frame. Apply double-sided tape to the frame, slightly covering the edges of the plastic. Remove the liner from the tape.

7 *Finish the card.* Layer the framed acetate on a square notecard.

The finished card.

Dreamy Face

What you'll need:

- face stamp from Rubber Zone
- permanent ink
- acetate
- Diamond Glaze
- glitter
- dye re-inkers
- scissors
- tissue paper
- brayer (or other smooth cylindrical object)
- notecard

This underglazing technique puts the acetate's paper liner to work.

1 *Stamp, glaze and apply glitter.* On this card, the image of the face was stamped in permanent ink first. Once the design is dry, turn the plastic over and pour on the Diamond Glaze. Then add your ink. Spread the mixture over the surface of the plastic. Do not go all the way out to the edge of the plastic—leave at least a ½" margin around the edge. While the mixture is still very wet, sprinkle on a medium grind of glitter.

T I P

✄ You can use printed tissues for added interest. Also try crinkling the tissue for a textured look.

2 *Apply tissue.* Lay the piece of liner tissue over the entire mixture.

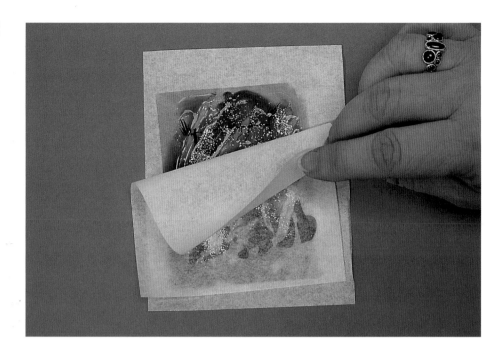

3 *Roll with brayer.* With a rubber brayer, slowly and gently roll over the tissue, sealing the plastic and tissue together. Doing this allows you to work with the piece sooner than allowing it to dry on its own because the tissue absorbs much of the liquid.

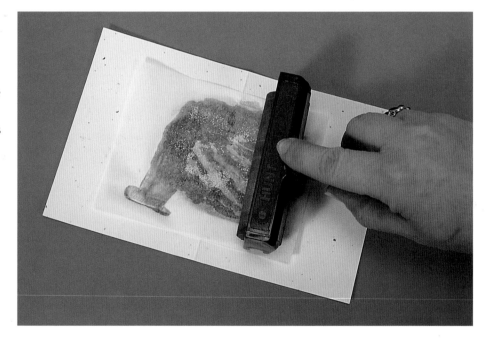

TIP

✯ For a smooth look, use the brayer. If you like more texture, simply lay the tissue on the glaze and pat the surface of the tissue down.

4 *Trim the acetate.* In 5 to 10 minutes the piece should be ready to cut. Test the piece for dryness by touching the tissue. Cut the piece down to approximately 3¼" x 4". Trim away the excess.

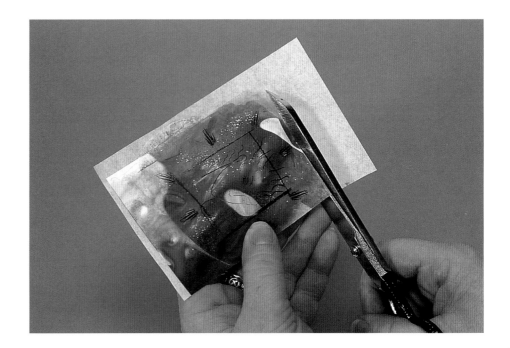

5 *Apply acetate to card.* Apply a few drops of Diamond Glaze to the tissue side of the piece and spread the glaze well. Adhere the piece to the front of a notecard.

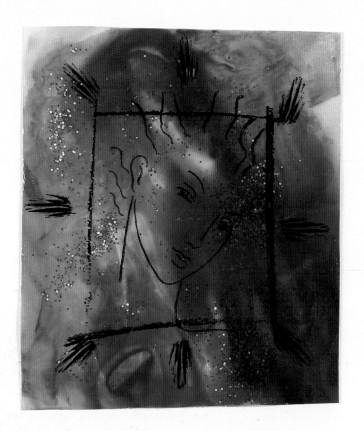

The finished card.

Elegant Women

What you'll need:

- stamp by JudiKins
- dye re-inkers
- brown kraft cardstock
- gold embossing powder
- craft knife
- Diamond Glaze
- small paintbrush
- paper cords
- tall notecard
- white colored pencil

Another idea to try with Diamond Glaze is to mix it with dye re-inkers and then use it as a translucent paint. I call this technique "overglazing."

1 *Emboss your image.* Emboss an image in gold on brown kraft cardstock. This image is long, so I cut it into three separate images.

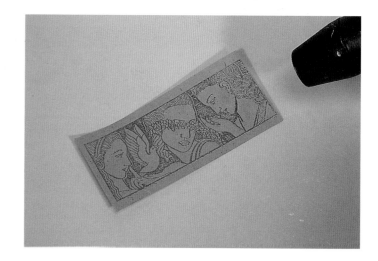

2 *Mix glaze and paint image.* Mix one drop of each color dye with five drops of Diamond Glaze in a paint tray or small plastic dish. Paint the images, being careful to keep the glazing mixture off of the gold embossing. The dove in the second section should be white, so I used a white pencil on it.

3 *Create the cord border.* While the pieces are drying, create the border strip by cutting a piece of double-sided masking tape ½" wide and at least 8½" long. Cover the tape with paper cord, starting at the center and working out.

4 *Finish the card.* Attach the stamped images to the left side of the front of a tall card. Remove the liner from the tape and lay the border as shown.

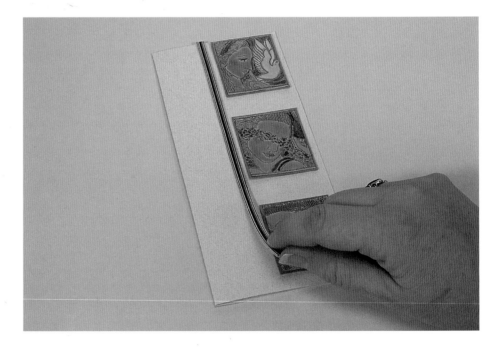

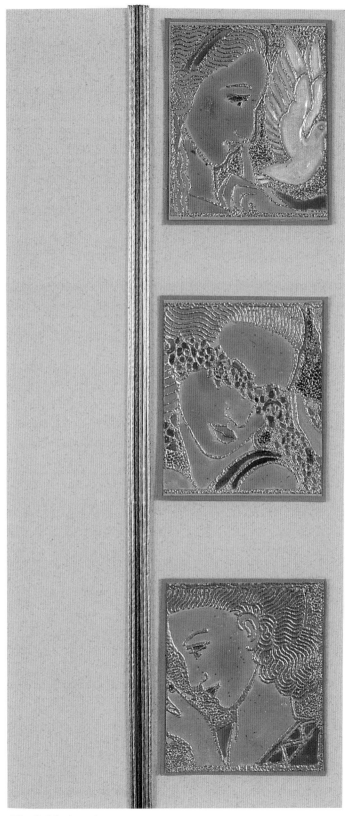

The finished card.

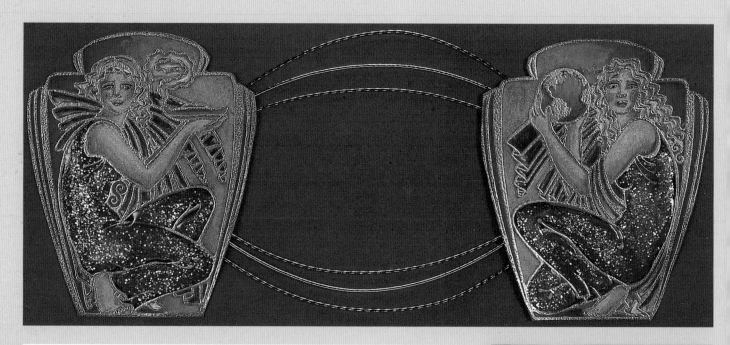

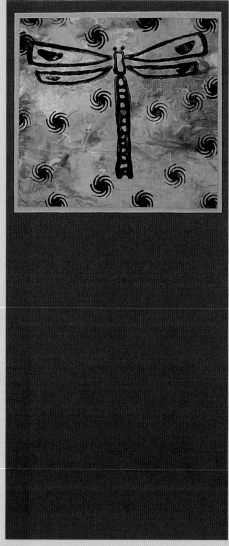

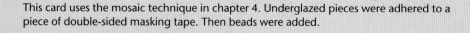
This card uses the mosaic technique in chapter 4. Underglazed pieces were adhered to a piece of double-sided masking tape. Then beads were added.

I usually stamp my image on the front of the acetate, but you can also stamp on the back. Remember that your image will be reversed if you stamp on the back of the acetate.

I stamped and overglazed the image of the woman, then cut it out and placed it over an underglazed panel.

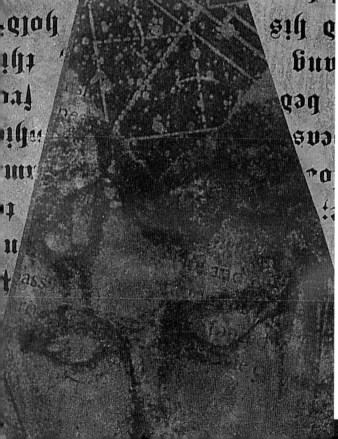

CHAPTER

6

(STAMPS CLOCKWISE FROM LEFT) Zettiology, Acey Duecy, Zettiology.

collage veneers

This is an interesting technique you might recognize. Many people who create their own overhead-projector transparencies use this method. The technique can also be used to create greeting cards or in building a collage. It is relatively simple, which makes it very fun and a great project for kids as well as adults.

WE ARE SHAPED AND FASHIONED BY WHAT WE LOVE

Holiday Card

What you'll need:

- snowflake stamp by JudiKins
- color photocopy in a design of your choice
- heavy clear self-adhesive laminate or acetate
- bone folder
- craft knife or scissors
- bowl of water big enough to hold laminate
- square notecard
- metallic gel ink pen
- double-sided clear tape
- double-sided foam tape
- copy of a small vintage photograph

This process transfers an image from paper to the adhesive side of heavy clear acetate or laminate. You will get the best results using photocopies (color or black and white) because the paper is thin and does not take long to remove from the adhesive. Magazines and many other printed materials will work, but can take longer. Ink jet printers do not work! Here I have started with a color copy of an old piece of holiday fabric. The copy was cut to 4" x 4".

Once you've tried this project, try collaging several images together directly on the sticky side of the laminate. Apply metallic pens, powdered pigments or gold leaf foils to the sticky side of the acetate for a dramatic effect.

1 *Adhere copy to laminate.* Apply the copy to the sticky side of a piece of heavy clear laminate.

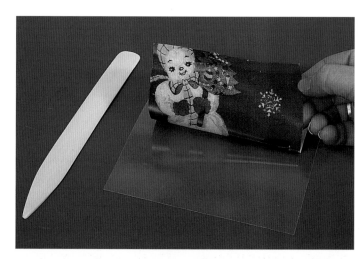

2 *Burnish.* Carefully burnish the back side of the copy with a bone folder or brayer.

3 *Trim.* Trim any excess laminate.

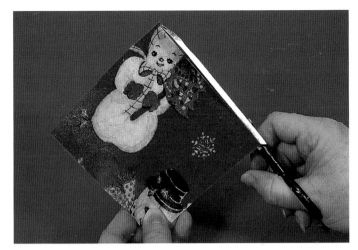

4 *Immerse in water.* Immerse the entire piece in plain water for 3 minutes.

5 *Rub off the paper.* Place the piece on paper towels face (shiny side) down. Begin rubbing the paper off the laminate with the tips of your fingers. It is very important not to use a sharp object to do the rubbing because it could scrape the veneer. Be sure to remove as much paper as possible. If you see a feltlike residue when the piece is dry, dip the piece in water again and continue rubbing.

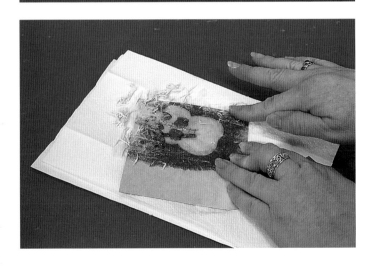

TIP

✮ Keep your fingers wet when rubbing off the paper. This helps speed the removal process.

The finished veneer should be translucent when all the paper is rubbed off. Notice that the portion that was white is now clear.

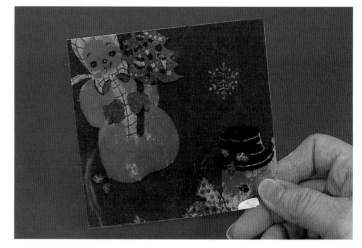

6 *Stamp.* Stamp a border around a square card.

7 *Create a metallic border.* I used a metallic gel ink pen to trace a border on the notecard around the trimmed laminate.

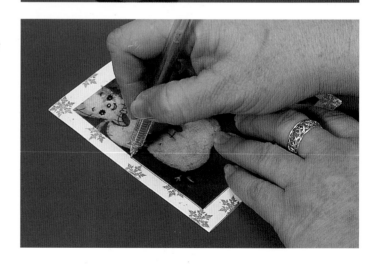

8 *Finish.* Finish the card by using clear double-sided tape to adhere the small photocopy of a vintage photograph to the veneer. To create a 3-D effect, I used double-sided foam tape squares to adhere the veneer to the card. You can also use clear double-sided tape.

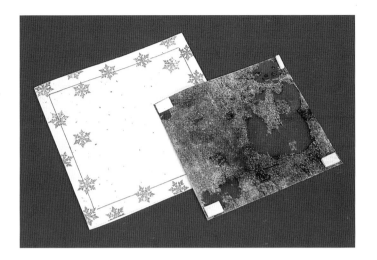

The finished card.

The card at the left incorporates a picture of my grandmother and aunt. The background of the card above is made up of old advertising. I added the Hotel Victoria image and the cancelled stamp image.

The background of the card above is a collage of images from a magazine. I added the Eiffel Tower stamp (which is from Carmen's Veranda).

You can add a variety of materials to the adhesive side of the laminate in order to create some stunning special effects. Try powdered pigments, metallic paint pens and gold leaf. Add a few drops of Diamond Glaze for a very modern metal look.

The card above was made with a black and white photocopy of an image of an angel given to me by Zelda of Cleveland. I have photo-copied it so many times that the picture has become grainy. I really like that effect.

CHAPTER

7

(STAMPS CLOCKWISE FROM LEFT) Stampers Anonymous, Paper Parachute, JudiKins.

pastels
and
crayons

Remember the feeling of new crayons in your hand? Experience the joy of simple coloring and messy fingers with water-soluble crayons and pastel chalks.

Basic Pastel Background

What you'll need:

- passion flower stamp by Stamp Camp
- pastel sticks
- craft knife
- uncoated (not glossy) postcard
- sponge
- pigment ink pad
- embossing powder
- heat gun
- double-sided tape

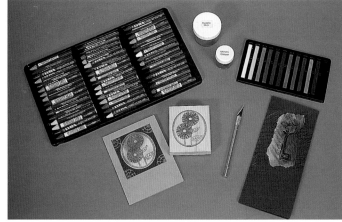

Materials, clockwise from top left: water-soluble crayons, metallic embossing powders, pastel sticks, craft knife, stamp.

Some of the most fun I have with stamping is with water-soluble crayons and regular chalk pastels. They are easy to use on many surfaces and are quick to clean up since they don't stain your fingers!

1 *Scrape the pastel stick.* Scrape the pastel stick with a craft knife, allowing the dust to fall onto an uncoated postcard.

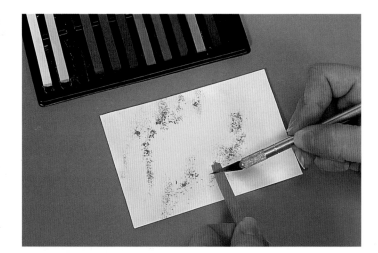

2 *Smear the pastel dust.* Smear the dust into the paper with your fingers or a sponge. Add several more colors in the same manner, blending as you go. Carefully blow away the excess chalk.

TIP

✺ Begin with the lightest color in the center and then blend with medium and darker colors.

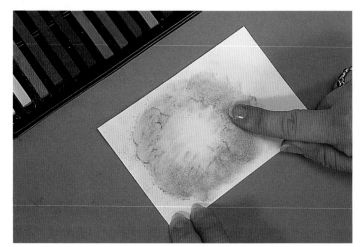

3 *Stamp the image.* Stamp a favorite image onto the paper with pigment ink.

4 *Apply embossing powder.* Pour on a dark embossing powder such as Galaxy. Shake off the excess.

5 *Melt the powder.* Use a heat gun to melt the powder.

6 *Finish the card.* Trim the excess paper from the edge of the image and then use double-sided tape to adhere the finished part to a tall notecard.

Simple Watercolor Wash

What you'll need:

- water-soluble crayons
- uncoated postcard
- water
- small paintbrush

Water-soluble crayons are simple and fun to use. Create watercolor washes for backgrounds or to color in stamped designs. They work on most kinds of paper and can be permanently fixed with a matte spray fixative or even hairspray.

This is a great way to do quick backgrounds for stamping landscapes.

1 *Apply color.* In the center of a postcard scribble a section of color, and then a section of a contrasting color.

2 *Add water.* Spritz generously with water. Allow to dry.

3 *Blend.* Try blending the colors together while wet for a smoother look. Use these postcards to create background layers for notecards, or stamp large designs over the colors once they have completely dried.

Artful View Card

What you'll need:

- face stamp by JudiKins
- water-soluble crayons
- black dye ink pad
- water
- small paintbrush
- paper
- square notecard

1 *Stamp the face.* Begin by inking a large face stamp with black dye ink. Stamp the face.

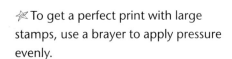

TIP

★ To get a perfect print with large stamps, use a brayer to apply pressure evenly.

2 *Apply color.* Apply the crayons in a variety of colors around—but not over—the face design. Carefully apply color to the eyes and lips.

3 *Blend the colors.* With a small amount of water on a paintbrush, gently blend the outside colors in toward the center, but not over the face. Rinse the brush and squeeze out most of the water. Blend the color on the eyes and lips. Follow the shading of the stamp design for shadows. Once the piece is dry, apply small dabs of white crayon to the whites of the eyes and as a highlight in the irises. This makes the face light up and stand out against the background.

4 *Tear the paper.* Tear away the edges of the paper and apply it to a deeper shade of paper with double-sided tape. Tear the edges of this second piece of paper slowly. Tearing the paper toward you will leave a rough appearance on the front of the piece; alternating tearing toward you and away from you can give an interesting texture to the collage. Add tape to the back of the deeper paper and layer the whole piece onto a square notecard. Finish it off with a tassel.

TIP

✷ For a glossy appearance, try spreading Diamond Glaze over the piece and then adding a small amount of glitter.

Fun Face Card

What you'll need:

- stamps by Paula Best
- pigment ink pad
- embossing powder heat gun
- water-soluble crayons
- water
- small paintbrush
- double-sided masking tape

1 *Stamp the background.* Stamp a background with a fun word stamp. Here I have used two light shades of dye inks. Don't use more than three colors; limiting the colors will keep the pattern harmonious.

2 *Stamp the face.* Stamp the large face stamp using a pigment ink.

3 *Add embossing powder.* Cover the image in embossing powder and then shake off the excess.

4 *Heat powder.* Heat the powder thoroughly and allow the piece to cool.

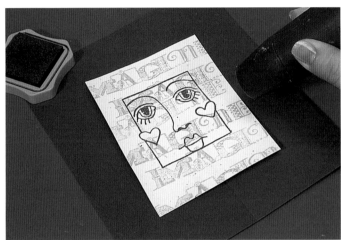

5 *Color.* Color in the open sections of the stamps with colors similar to those used in the background.

6 *Blend.* With a slightly damp paintbrush, blend the crayon colors.

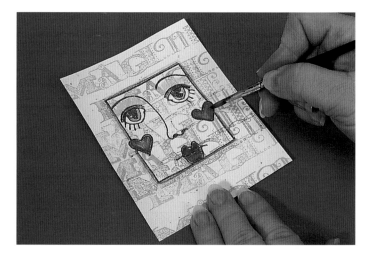

7 *Add more color.* Add a rim of green around the outside edge of the face stamp and then blend that out with a bit more water.

8 *Finish.* When the piece has dried, trim off any excess and apply to a notecard with double-sided tape.

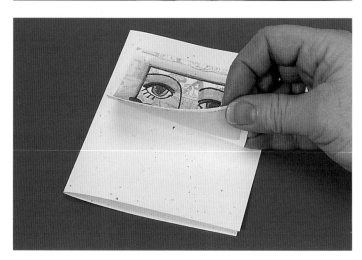

The finished card. I like to add the texture of a soft background to an open image like this face. It gives the card more interest, especially when you hve a simple white card as your base.

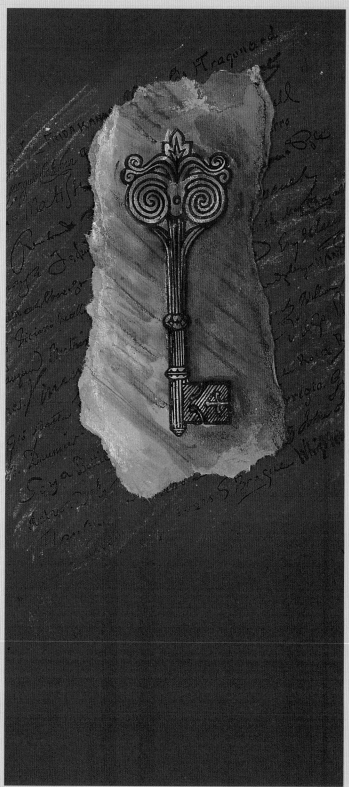

Use colored pencil to add even more detail.

I stamped this image and colored it with crayons, being careful to blend loosely. Don't overdo it.

After stamping the words and the face, I added color by smudging pastels.

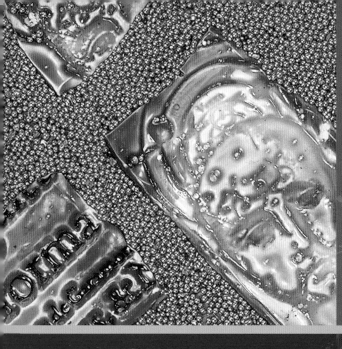

PEARS · PEARS · PEARS · PEARS
bartlett · anjou · asian · winter nelis · bo
dumont · kieffer · forelle · rogue red · comic
honeysweet · seckel · grand champion · aur
...am's triumph · bartle
...e · grand champion · a

(STAMPS CLOCKWISE FROM LEFT) JudiKins, A Stamp in the Hand, A Stamp in the Hand

shrink plastic

Shrink plastic came out as a kids' craft item in the late 1960s. It was fun for kids—and easy to use because the images came preprinted on the plastic. With rubber stamps you can create your own images or scenes to shrink. Practice makes perfect with shrink plastic, so be sure you have enough on hand to play with. Always stamp a few extra images to use as charms. This stuff is fun!

Abstract Elegance

What you'll need:

- swirl stamps by Paula Best
- white or translucent shrink plastic
- heat gun (or oven)
- translucent gold embossing powder
- craft knife or scissors
- glass beads

- two colors of metallic pigment ink
- white and dark-purple cardstock
- black corrugated paper
- paper cord
- double-sided masking tape

There are many kinds of shrink plastics out there: white, super clear, translucent (or frosted) and black. There are even some colored varieties. I prefer the super clear for many of my projects because it has a glasslike finish once it is heated.

Permanent ink is the best on plastic since it does not run or bead up. If you want to add color, you can use colored pencils. On translucent or white plastic you may want to sand the surface lightly with an emery board before coloring. This adds some tooth to the surface, and the plastic will accept the colored pencils more easily. Be sure to sand in both directions so the plastic will shrink evenly. Super clear can be stamped on one side and colored on the reverse with water-based metallic markers.

Shrink plastic shrinks down to 40 to 50 percent of the original size. The oven is absolutely the best method for heating and shrinking the plastic. Follow the directions on the package for oven temperature and time. You can also use a heat gun, but this method is sometimes tricky. Be sure to practice!

This project is good for a beginner because it doesn't matter if the plastic is bumpy or doesn't lie flat.

1 *Tear the plastic.* Tear a piece of white or translucent shrink plastic into an unusual shape approximately 2" x 2".

T I P

✮ You can use a hold punch to cut ⅛" holes before shrinking to create jewelry pieces or charms for cards.

---

2 *Shrink it.* Shrink the piece with a heat gun. Don't worry if the piece is bumpy or doesn't flatten out completely.

3 *Add embossing powder.* Cover the warm plastic with embossing powder and shake off the excess. Here I have used Translucent Gold.

4 *Heat the powder.* Use the heat gun to melt the embossing powder.

5 *Add glass beads.* While the powder is in a liquid state, sprinkle on a few colored glass beads.

TIP

✳ Try adding glitter instead of beads to the hot embossing powder for a brilliant sheen.

6 *Reheat.* Reheat the whole piece lightly to seal everything together.

7 *Stamp your card.* Set the piece aside to cool. For the card, stamp two colors of metallic pigment ink on a white and dark-purple piece of cardstock.

8 *Cut the card.* Cut the dark-purple cardstock down to 4½" x 3½". Cut a piece of 3½" x 2½" black corrugated paper. Punch two ⅟₁₆" holes in the corrugated paper approximately 1" apart, as shown. Thread the paper cord through the holes and tie on the abstract piece of plastic.

9 *Layer.* Layer all the parts together with double-sided masking tape.

Catalina Tiles

What you'll need:

- border stamp by Paper Parachute
- white shrink plastic
- craft knife or scissors
- heat gun
- several colors of dye re-inkers
- Diamond Glaze
- small paintbrush
- powdered pigment
- double-sided masking tape
- copper embossing powder

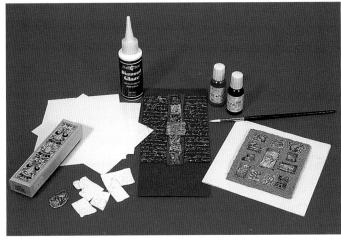

Materials, clockwise from upper left: stamp, shrink plastic, Diamond Glaze, dye re-inkers, paintbrush.

Here is an easy and fun alternative to stamping an image on the plastic. These tiles can be used for jewelry or as embellishments on cards or boxes. This is also a great technique for decorating small box lids.

1 *Cut and shrink tiles.* Cut small squares of white shrink plastic of various sizes. Irregular shapes work well too and have the appearance of broken tile. Shrink the pieces with a heat gun until they become flat.

2 *Stamp.* Quickly impress a stamp image into the hot plastic. Make up several of these pieces before moving on to the next step.

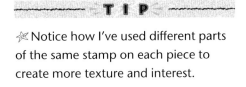

T I P

✭ Notice how I've used different parts of the same stamp on each piece to create more texture and interest.

3 *Make colors.* Make glazes of three or four different colors by adding a drop of dye re-inker to a nickel-size dollop of Diamond Glaze.

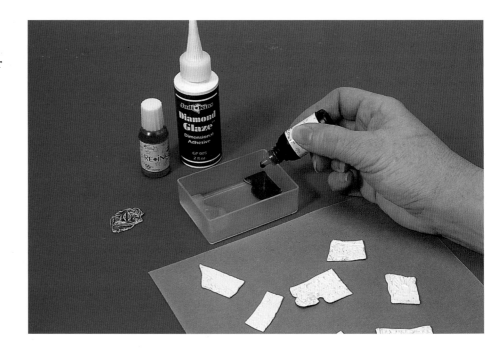

4 *Paint the tiles.* Paint the tiles starting with the lightest color, adding dots or highlighting edges using the darker colors in different parts of each tile.

5 *Add powdered pigment.* If you like a metallic finish, add a little powdered pigment with your paintbrush while the tiles are still wet.

T I P

✯ Powdered pigments come in a wide range of colors and are available at stamp and craft stores. These pigments must be mixed with a liquid like Diamond Glaze or acrylic medium to adhere to surfaces. If applied in their powdered state, a spray fixative should be used to adhere them to the surface and prevent smearing.

---

6 *Apply embossing powder to tape.* While the tiles are drying, cut a 6" piece of double-sided masking tape. Lay the tape exposed side up and pour copper embossing powder over the entire surface.

7 *Heat.* Heat the powder and while it is hot, pour on another layer of copper powder. Repeat this step. Heat the piece completely and then set it aside to cool. The tiles must be completely dry and cool before the next step.

8 *Reheat.* Reheat the powder on the tape until it is very fluid. Carefully add the tiles onto the tape on top of the liquid embossing powder.

9 *Adhere tiles.* Press each tile down firmly. Adhere tiles on top of the base tiles with Diamond Glaze. Let dry.

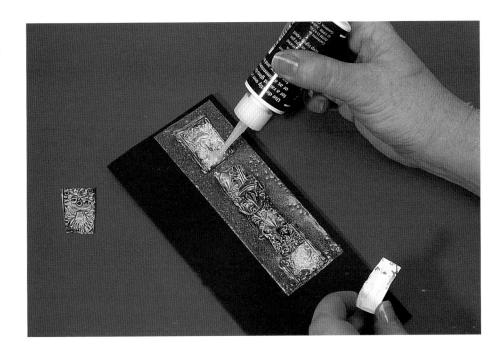

10 *Finish card.* Remove the backing from the tape and apply the tape directly to a tall card.

T I P

✶ To secure the tiles, be sure to allow some of the embossing powder to melt over the edges of the tile.

The finished card.

Beaded Tiles

What you'll need:

- stamp by Zettiology
- fifteen or more shrink plastic tiles
- heavy chipboard
- tray or box lid
- Diamond Glaze
- glass beads
- double-sided masking tape
- square notecard

This technique creates a very heavy card, but it is so intriguing you won't mind the extra postage. You can also try this technique on a cardboard picture frame. Before you begin, make up at least fifteen shrink plastic tiles and color them with the Diamond Glaze/re-inker mixtures described previously.

1 *Prepare the chipboard.* You'll need at least fifteen dry tiles. Place a 3½" x 3" piece of heavy chipboard in a small tray or box lid. Spread a thick layer of Diamond Glaze over the chipboard.

2 *Arrange the tiles.* Arrange the tiles in a pleasing pattern on top of the glaze. Leave space between each tile.

3 *Pour on the beads.* Pour glass beads over the glaze. Do not move the tray for at least 20 minutes.

<hr />

T I P

✯ If all your tiles are the same color, try sprinkling on a second color of beads while the glaze is still wet for more interest.

4 *Finish the card.* After the time has elapsed, shake off the excess beads. Apply the double-sided tape to the chipboard, then layer the piece onto a square note card. For this project I have layered two of these beaded pieces together.

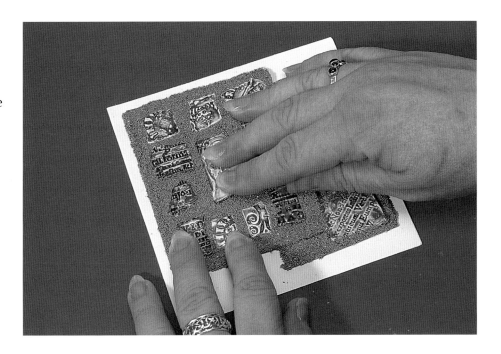

The finished card. If the chipboard starts to curl after you have applied the Diamond Glaze, don't worry. As you press in the tiles, the chipboard will relax.

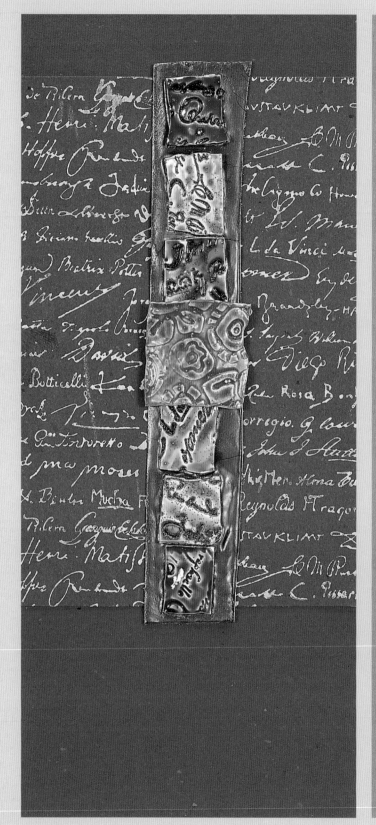

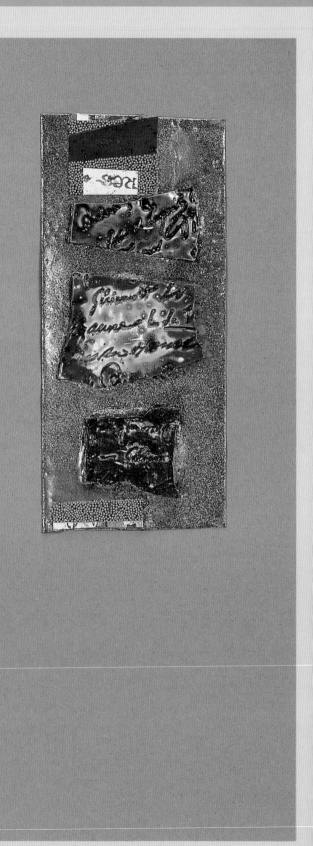

This design incorporates stamped paper.

These square pieces and the long rectangular piece were cut from wood veneer that you can find at most home centers.

CHAPTER

9

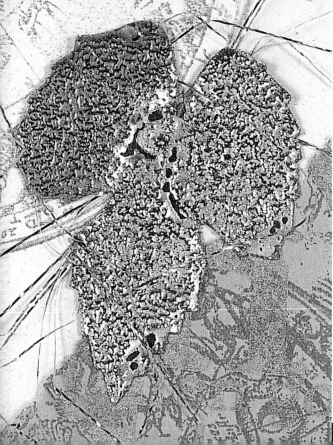

(STAMPS CLOCKWISE FROM LEFT) Acey Duecy, Toy Box, Stampers Anonymous.

natural adornments

Stones, leaves, shells, pods and bark—all of these natural elements can be used on your greeting cards. You can even stamp or emboss most of these surfaces. Slate works very well as a card embellishment because it is relatively thin and lightweight. It also embosses well for those same reasons. Leaves, seeds, bark and pods should be relatively flat. These elements cannot be too bulky or too heavy to attach to paper or board: It would make the card too difficult to mail in an envelope. Of course, you can solve the problem by sending the piece in another container, such as a box or a tube. Silk leaves can also be used in place of dried leaves for a more permanent display.

Silver Cups

What you'll need:

- embossing ink
- small dried flowers
- paper towels
- silver embossing powder
- heat gun
- cancelled postage stamps
- double-sided tape
- scissors
- hole punch
- thin gold thread
- square notecard

Materials, clockwise from upper left: small tray, embossing ink, embossing powders, stamp, metallic ink pad, gold thread, small paintbrush, cancelled postage stamps, dried or silk flowers and leaves, hole punches.

Dried flowers are available everywhere—you probably have a few around the house. This is a great technique to use when they start looking a bit worn out. Pour your embossing ink into a small container for ease of use. (You can also roll sturdy flowers in pigment ink to add color.)

1 *Dip flowers in embossing ink.* Pour embossing ink into a small tray. Dip each flower into the embossing ink to coat.

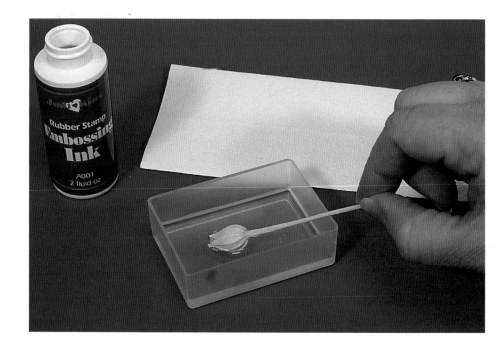

2 *Blot flower.* Blot each flower lightly to remove excess ink.

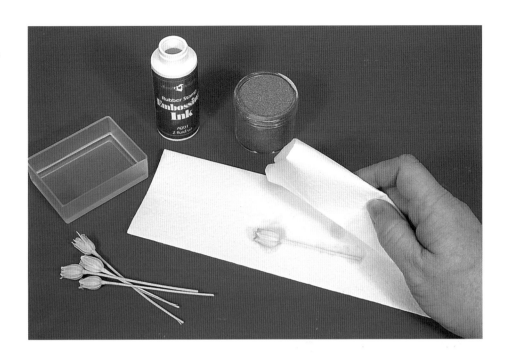

3 *Dip flowers in embossing powder.* Coat the flowers in silver embossing powder.

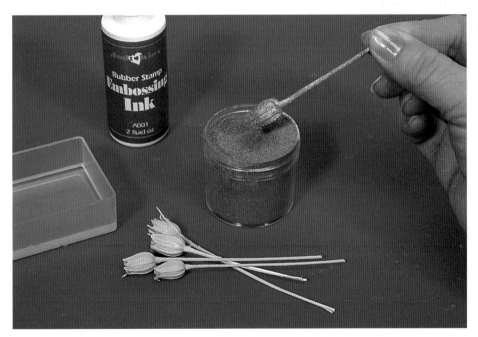

4 *Heat.* Heat the powder. If the flowers have long stems, and you are doing several at once, stick them into a stiff foam block. Don't get the heat gun too close to the foam because it will melt.

5 *Create the card.* Set the flowers aside. Affix cancelled postage stamps to one side of double-sided masking tape. Trim the edges away with scissors.

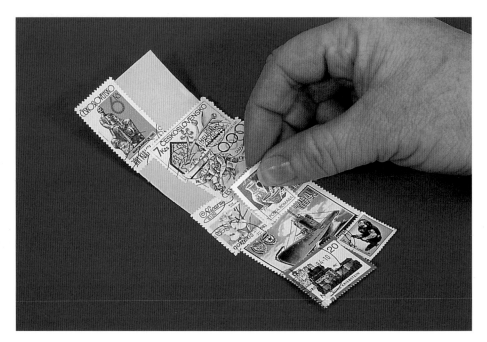

6 *Punch holes.* Punch two small holes about ¼" apart in the center of the tape.

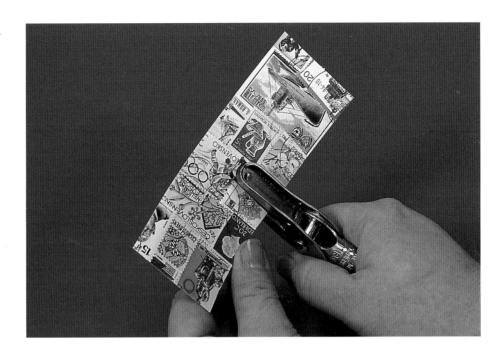

7 *Tie on flowers.* Use decorative gold thread to tie on the silver-cup flowers.

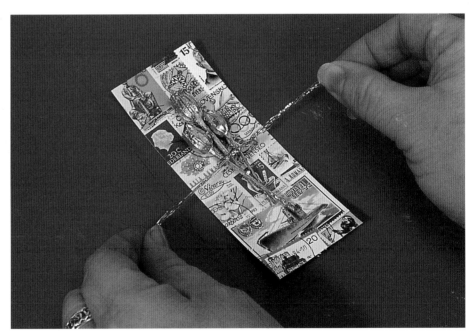

8 *Finish card.* Remove the backing from the tape and adhere the tape directly to a square notecard.

The finished card.

Worldly Leaf

What you'll need:

- zodiac stamp by Toy Box
- large word stamp by Stampers Anonymous
- silk or dry leaf
- embossing ink
- silver embossing powder
- translucent gold embossing powder
- paper towels
- heat gun
- cardstock in sage green and gray-green
- white postcard
- deep-green dye ink
- gold pigment ink
- double-sided masking tape
- natural fibers

If you plan to use silk leaves, be sure to remove the plastic stems before embossing.

The greatest success in embossing leaves is usually achieved with a sturdy dry leaf or a silk leaf. Of course, the older the leaf, the greater the chance it will fall apart. I like to use real leaves for temporary items such as centerpieces or other decorations. For greeting cards it is easier to use silk leaves.

1 *Dip leaves in embossing ink.* For this project we will be embossing with two different powders, Silver and Translucent Gold. Dip the leaf into embossing ink and then blot off any excess.

2 *Add embossing powder.* Pour silver powder on half of the leaf. Shake off the excess and return the remainder to the jar.

3 *Repeat.* Repeat the process with Translucent Gold on the other half of the leaf.

4 *Heat.* Heat the powder and then set the leaf aside to cool.

5 *Assemble the card.* To create the card you'll need a sage green square card, a white postcard and a piece of gray-green cardstock. Tear the gray-green cardstock diagonally as shown. Stamp this piece several times with the zodiac stamp in deep-green dye ink.

6 *Stamp.* Stamp the large word stamp over the same piece with gold pigment ink. On the white postcard, stamp the zodiac stamp once in the corner.

7 *Build the card.* Affix the cards to the sage square card with double-sided tape as shown. Apply the same tape to the back of the leaf.

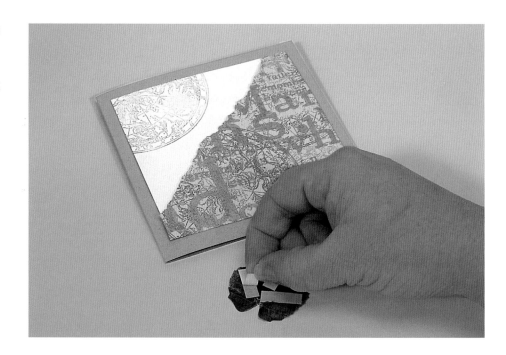

8 *Place leaf.* Lay the leaf down lightly for placement.

9 *Add fibers underneath.* Lift half of the leaf up and tuck a few fibers under it. Reposition the leaf and apply pressure to the entire leaf.

The finished card.

Stone Tablets

What you'll need:

- handwriting stamp by JudiKins
- leaf stamp by Rubber Monger
- small, flat piece of slate
- metallic pigment ink
- gold embossing powder
- heat gun
- black corrugated paper
- Diamond Glaze
- double-sided tape
- cardstock
- notecard

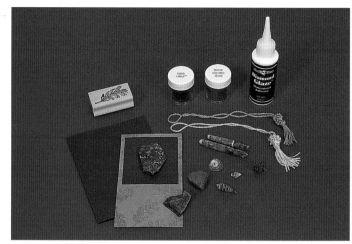

Materials, clockwise from upper left: stamp, embossing powder, Diamond Glaze, tassels, shells, dried flowers and small rocks.

Small pebbles and slate can be very effective on cards. Slate works very well because it is flat.

1 *Stamp the slate.* Here I am using a small piece of slate. Ink the stamp with a metallic pigment ink and lay the stone on the stamp.

2 *Add embossing powder.* Pour on the gold powder.

3 *Heat.* Heat the stone carefully. It takes longer to emboss rocks because of the density, so be sure to emboss on a heat-resistant surface.

TIP

✯ Your cutting mat is not heat resistant, so don't use your heat gun too close to it.

4 *Glue stone to paper.* Attach the stone to a piece of black corrugated paper with a dab of Diamond Glaze. Allow the piece to dry thoroughly.

5 *Finish the card.* Use double-sided tape to apply the stone and black paper to a layer of stamped cardstock. Finish by layering onto a notecard and wrapping gold thread through and around the card fold.

Sea Shells

What you'll need:

- stamp by JudiKins
- small sea shells
- pigment ink or embossing ink
- bronze embossing powder
- heat gun

You can emboss sea shells just like slate. Attach shells to tassels or use them as central ornaments. To attach to thread, drill a small hole in the shell before inking and embossing.

1 *Ink shells.* Try to roll long shells across the stamp.

2 *Emboss.* Roll the shells in bronze embossing powder and heat.

For this card, holes were drilled in the long shells before they were stamped (you can purchase some types of shells pre-drilled), then cords were run through the holes once the shells had cooled from the heat gun. A square scrap of stamped paper provided the foundation for a spiral shell that I had immersed in embossing ink and embossing powder and then heated.

The edges of the eucalyptus bark were coated with the same metallic pen used on the edges of the paper.

This face was stamped on a broken piece of wood veneer. You could also use tree bark or stained balsa wood.

The shells on both of these cards were secured with layers of melted embossing powder, then coated with Amazing Glaze for a clear finish. The card on the right has colored powders incorporated into the Amazing Glaze. Glitter and beads can also be added.

Resources

stamp companies

The companies listed in this directory sell high-quality rubber stamps. All the companies listed have different policies regarding copyrights, catalogs, stamps and supplies. Many companies now have Web sites you can visit.

ACEY DUECY
P.O. Box 194
Ancram, NY 12502

ALICE IN RUBBERLAND
P.O. Box 9262
Seattle, WA 98109

AMERICAN ART STAMP
3892 Del Amo Blvd. Suite 701
Torrance, CA 90503
(310) 371-6593
Fax 310-371-5545

ART GONE WILD
3110 Payne Ave.
Cleveland, OH 44114
(800) 945-3950
artgwild@aol.com

CARMEN'S VERANDA/POSTSCRIPT
P.O. Box 1539
Placentia, CA 92871
(888) 227-6367
http://www.carmensveranda.com

CLAUDIA ROSE
15 Baumgarten Road
Saugerties, NY 12477
(914) 679-9235

COFFEE BREAK DESIGNS
P.O. Box 34281
Indianapolis, IN 46234
coffeebreakdesign@ameritech.net

**THE CREATIVE BLOCK/
STAMPERS ANONYMOUS**
20613 Center Ridge Road
Rocky River, OH 44116
(440) 333-7941

CURTIS UYEDA/CURTIS' COLLECTION
3326 St. Michael Drive
Palo Alto, CA 94306

DENAMI DESIGN
P.O. Box 5617
Kent, WA 98064
(253) 639-2546

DRAGGIN' INK
P.O. Box 24135
Santa Barbara, CA 93121
(805) 966-5297

FEBRUARY PAPER
P.O. Box 4297
Olympia, WA 98501
(360) 705-1519

GUMBALL GRAPHICS
1417 Creighton Ave.
Dayton, OH 45420
(513) 258-2663

HOT POTATOES
2805 Columbine Place
Nashville, TN 37204
(615) 269-8002
http://www.hotpotatoes.com

JUDIKINS
17803 S. Harvard Blvd
Gardena, CA 90248
(310) 515-1115
http://www.judikins.com

LOVE YOU TO BITS/TIN CAN MAIL
P.O. Box 5748
Redwood City, CA 94063
(800) 546-LYTB

MAGENTA
351 Blain, Mont-Saint-Hilaire
Quebec, Canada J3H3B4
(514) 446-5253

MEER IMAGE
P.O. Box 12
Arcata, CA 95518
http://www.meerimage.com

MOE WUBBA
P.O. Box 1445, Dept. B
San Luis Obispo, CA 93406
(805) 547-1MOE

PAM BAKKE PASTE PAPERS
303 Highland Dr.
Bellingham, WA 98225
(360) 738-4830

PAPER PARACHUTE
P.O. Box 91385
Portland, OR 97291-0385

RUBBER BABY BUGGY BUMPERS
1331 W. Mountain Ave.
Fort Collins, CO 80521
(970) 224-3499
http://www.rubberbaby.com

RUBBER MONGER
P.O. Box 1777
Snowflake, AZ 85937
Fax: (888) 9MONGER

RUBBERMOON
P.O. Box 3258
Hayden Lake, ID 83835
(208) 772-9772

RUBBER ZONE
P.O. Box 10254
Marina del Rey, CA 90295
http://www.rubberzone.com

RUBY RED RUBBER
P.O. Box 2076
Yorba Linda, CA 92885
(714) 970-7584

SKYCRAFT DESIGNS
26395 S. Morgan Rd.
Estacada, OR 97023
(503) 630-7173

STAMPACADABRA
5091 N Fresno St. Suite 133
Fresno, CA 93710
(209) 227-7247

STAMP CAMP
P.O. Box 222091
Dallas, TX 75222
(214) 330-6831

STAMPSCAPES
7451 Warner Ave. #E124
Huntington Beach, CA 92647

STAMPS HAPPEN, INC
369 S. Acacia Ave.
Fullerton, CA 92631
(714) 879-9894

A STAMP IN THE HAND
20630 S. Leapwood Ave. Suite B
Carson, CA 90746
(310) 329-8555
http://www.astampinthehand.com

**STAMP YOUR ART OUT/
ENVELOPES PLEASE**
9685 Kenwood Rd.
Cincinnati, OH 45242
(513) 793-4558

THE STUDIO
PO Box 5681
Bellevue, WA 98006

TOYBOX RUBBER STAMPS
P.O. Box 1487
Healdsburg, CA 95448
(707) 431-1400

TWENTY-TWO
6167 North Broadway, No. 322
Chicago, IL 60660

VIVA LAS VEGASTAMPS
1008 East Sahara Ave.
Las Vegas, NV 89104
(702) 836-9118

WORTH REPEATING
227 N. East St.
New Auburn, WI 54757
(715) 237-2011

ZETTIOLOGY/THE STUDIO
P.O. Box 5681
Bellevue, WA 98006

publications

For more information (including stamp-related Web sites) on stamping or stores in your area, try these stamping publications:

THE RUBBERSTAMPER
225 Gordons Corner Road
P.O. Box 420
Manalapan, NJ 07726-0420
(800) 969-7176

RUBBERSTAMPMADNESS
408 SW Monroe #210
Corvallis, OR 97330
(541) 752-0075

RUBBERSTAMP SOURCEBOOK & TRAVELERS GUIDE TO RUBBERSTAMPING
Cornucopia Press
4739 University Way NE
Suite 1610-A
Seattle, WA 98105
(206) 528-8120

STAMPER'S SAMPLER & SOMERSET STUDIO
22992 Millcreek, Suite B
Laguna Hills, CA
(714) 380-7318

VAMP STAMP NEWS
P.O. BOX 386
Hanover, MD 21076-0386

favorite products

My favorite rubber-stamping products are listed below.

COLORBOX
pigment inks

DRAGGIN' INK
embossing powders

ENCORE
pigment inks

ENVELOPES PLEASE
diorama template

FEBRUARY PAPERS
decorative threads and yarns

JUDIKINS
card stock
detachable brayer
embossing powders
Amazing Glaze
Diamond Glaze
permanent ink
paper cord
tassels
glass beads
Wax Wafers
envelope templates

shrink plastic
acetate
laminating sheets
mosaic tape

LYRA
watercolor crayons
pastel chalks

MARVY
dye inks

PAM BAKKE PASTE PAPERS
specialty papers

PEARL EX
powdered pigments

SCOTCH
double-sided cellophane tape
double-sided foam mounting tape

SKYCRAFT DESIGNS
specialty papers

SPEEDBALL
C-thru ruler
detachable brayer

stamps used in this book

Here is a list of all the stamps used in this book.

PAGE 6, planeterium by Toy Box, wave woman by Stampers Anonymous, script by A Stamp in the Hand. **PAGE 7**, clown girl by Zettiology. **PAGE 10**, butterfly woman by Stampers Anonymous, chair by Rubber Moon, script background by Zettiology, tiny wax seal by JudiKins. **PAGE 15**, butterfly woman by Stampers Anonymous. **PAGE 16**, deco cube by JudiKins. **PAGE 18**, sentiment by Zettiology. **PAGE 19**, Japanese mum and bird of paradise by Stamp Camp, tiny swirl by Twenty Two, paula best cubes by JudiKins. **PAGE 20**, large print background by Stampers Anonymous, statue by Toy Box, fish background by American Art Stamp, "Queen of Last Minute" by Paper Parachute, keys and crown by JudiKins. **PAGE 21**, bugs by Meer Image, clown girl by Zettiology. **PAGE 22**, dogs by Rubber Zone. **PAGE 27**, large print background by Stampers Anonymous, statue by Toy Box, bugs by Meer Image. **PAGE 28**, stars by paula best, chair by Rubber Moon, kissing couple by Curtis Uyeda. **PAGE 29**, oranges by Stamp Camp, deco panel by JudiKins. **PAGE 30**, deco panel by JudiKins. **PAGE 34-38**, stamps by paula best. **PAGE 39**, sun by A Stamp in the Hand, kissing couple by Curtis Uyeda. **PAGE 40**, floral background by American Art Stamp, "corpus" by Stampers Anonymous. **PAGE 48**, wave woman by Stampers Anonymous. **PAGE 50-51**, baroque,

origami, relish, deco swirls backgrounds by JudiKins. **PAGE 52**, three sisters, Lisa face, deco woman by JudiKins; pear by Stampers Anonymous; words by Zettiology. **PAGE 53**, dreamy lady by Rubber Zone, deco lady by JudiKins. **PAGE 56-58**, pear by Stampers Anonymous, words by Zettiology. **PAGE 60-62**, dreamy lady by Rubber Zone. **PAGE 63-65**, three sisters by JudiKins. **PAGE 66**, wishing and hoping deco ladies by JudiKins, dragonfly by Hot Potatoes, tiny swirl by Meer Image. **PAGE 67**, deco lady, Lisa face, square swirl by JudiKins; moon face by Rubber Moon. **PAGE 68-69**, Madrid, Eiffel tower by Carmen's Veranda; book by Acey Duecy; moon dial, "we are shaped" by Zettiology. **PAGE 72**, snowflake by JudiKins. **PAGE 74**, row of chairs by A Stamp in the Hand; cancellation, world tour background by Carmen's Veranda. **PAGE 75**, Eiffel tower by Carmen's Veranda. **PAGE 76**, flowers by Paper Parachute; butterflies background, Lisa face, artists' signatures by JudiKins; clock face by Stampers Anonymous. **PAGE 77**, heart face, "imagine" by paula best; three sisters by JudiKins. **PAGE 78**, flowers by Paper Parachute. **PAGE 79-80**, passion flower by Stamp Camp. Page **82-83**, Lisa face, artists' signatures by JudiKins. Page **84-87**, heart face, "imagine" by paula best. **PAGE 88**, willow, key butterflies by JudiKins. **PAGE 89**, artists' signatures, Mona face, deco cube by JudiKins; flowers by Paper Parachute; planeterium by Toy Box. **PAGE 90**, celestial woman by JudiKins, border by Paper Parachute, head by Zettiology, pears by A Stamp in the Hand. **PAGE 91**, pillar by A Stamp in the Hand. **PAGE 91-96**, paula best swirl cube by JudiKins. **PAGE 97-102**, border by Paper Parachute. **PAGE 103-105**, head, words by Zettiology. **PAGE 106-107**, artists' signatures, deco flowers by JudiKins; border by Paper Parachute. **PAGE 108**, world map by Toy Box, postoid by Acey Duecy. **PAGE 109**, leaf by Rubber Monger. **PAGE 117-119**, world map by Toy Box, large words by Stampers Anonymous. **PAGE 120-123**, leaf by Rubber Monger, artists' signatures by JudiKins. **PAGE 124**, paula best star cube by JudiKins, squared face by Rubber Moon. **PAGE 125**, swirl cube by JudiKins.

Index